The True Story of Bilbo the Surf Life

C000225579

~For My Mum in The Shetland Islands,
And all the children of the world ~ **Jmo**

~For my Dad and Mum,
And all the dogs of the world ~ **Jan**

First published 2008 by Cornish Cove Publishing

This First Edition published 2008

Layout design by Dom Elliott 01736 871114

Printed and bound by R Booth Ltd, Penryn, Cornwall 01326 373628

British Library Cataloguing in Publication Data
A catalogue record for this book is available from the British Library

ISBN   978-0-9550928-1-7

With thanks to photographer Colin Shepherd, Sennen Lifeguards, and the
children of Sennen School

Look out for Bilbo in action DVD

At a beach in Far West Cornwall, on mainland UK, one very experienced Head Lifeguard is the proud owner of a very special and highly skilled dog. They work together to protect swimmers and surfers from the dangers of the sea, to promote beach safety and the '*Swim Between the Flags*' campaign.

Bilbo accompanies Jmo in all his duties for The Lifeguard Service all year round, but they are mainly to be seen in action at the mile long beach of golden sand, the most westerly in the country, at Sennen Cove near Land's End.

Going in the sea is a fun thing to do, and it makes people smile and laugh and scream and shout with excitement. But the sea has its dangers too and to keep and eye on all the people on the beach and in the sea, there are lifeguards stationed at many of the busiest beaches around the whole coast of the British Isles. There are more lifeguards in Cornwall since, of all the counties, Cornwall has most beaches.

Lifeguards spend the day observing and looking through large binoculars at all the activity in the sea and around the water's edge, making sure everyone is being safe. Most days all is well and people have lots of fun at the beach — paddling, splashing around, swimming and surfing the breaking waves.

But the sea is a powerful force and it can overwhelm even the strongest of swimmers and most experienced surfer. At any moment the sea can change from being calm, to having a current that could sweep a person out to sea further than they want to go. This can be very frightening and even fatal, causing the person to drown.

Many people are rescued from the sea each year by Lifeguard teams. But only one team has a dog as a fully qualified member.

The following is the story of how Bilbo came to be a surf lifeguard.

Bilbo came to the Lifeguard service when he was a pup at 14 weeks old. At that time he belonged to the Beach Manager, who was also a friend of Jmo's. The Beach Manager had lots of meetings to attend and Bilbo was often left with Jmo back at the Lifeguard depot. Soon they became good friends.

As Bilbo grew larger and larger it became more difficult to bring him to the Lifeguard depot, because he needed more and more attention. So he was often left at home during the daytime and he became quite lonely.

It was around the time of Bilbo's second birthday (he was born on 5th May 2003), when Jmo happened to visit Bilbo's owners at their home. To Jmo's surprise Bilbo appeared to remember him, and was so excited upon seeing him, that he tried to jump the fence to get to Jmo. Bilbo had to be helped down because he got stuck! Jmo suggested to Bilbo's owners that he could go with him for a few days, to give him a break from the garden. They agreed and so Bilbo spent three days with Jmo, accompanying him in his duties around the West Cornwall coast inspecting the Static Buoyancy Aids, to check that they were in place and in working order. Bilbo clearly loved all the exercise, walking the coastal paths and driving to all the different coves.

But when Bilbo was returned to his home, he would not settle and howled all day and night. He would not eat and even had an upset tummy. His owners soon telephoned Jmo to see if he would like Bilbo to go and live with him permanently.

So it was that Bilbo came to live with Jmo in a small chalet overlooking the sea in deepest West Cornwall. And, because Jmo did not want his dog to be left alone again during the day, a condition was made that Bilbo could accompany Jmo to work each and every day, both on the beach in the summer and during other duties in the winter. Bilbo soon became happy again.

It was Bilbo's natural love of water that made Jmo realise that his new dog companion could be put to good use in the summer, promoting the 'Swim Between The Flags Campaign' down at the beach. Previously the Lifeguard Service had spent thousands of pounds putting signs up on beaches, advising people where to swim safely, but hardly anyone took any notice.

Jmo set about designing a jacket for Bilbo – his very own lifeguard jacket in the bright red and yellow lifeguard colours, with the safety message 'Swim Between The Flags' printed on it. The local 'Old Success Inn' sponsored Jmo by paying for the jacket to be made, and soon Bilbo was looking like a proper lifeguard. Bilbo proved an immediate hit with everyone especially children, really getting the message across to swim between the red and yellow flags.

Bilbo had to be put through some special swimming and fitness tests just like all the other lifeguards, such as learning how to swim in all types of sea conditions, negotiating the different surf and swim out beyond the breaking waves. He was soon swimming with skill and confidence, and rightly became a fully fledged member of the team himself — A fully qualified surf lifeguard dog — the world's first.

Since dogs are not allowed on Sennen beach during the summer months, Bilbo was trained to ride on the quad bike across the sand.

The quad stops at intervals so everyone can meet Bilbo and read what the message says on his jacket — *"Swim Between The Flags"*. Soon the phrase came about: '*Bilbo Says*', and now Bilbo even has his own web site called www.bilbosays.com

Bilbo sometimes has to ride on the Rescue Ski patrolling the deep water. He sits on the sled on the back, from where he can dive off to assist swimmers in trouble and tow them back to safety.

Bilbo has been trained to recognise when a person is in distress in the sea, and responds if someone is waving and shouting for help. He wears an harness onto which is clipped a Buoyancy Aid (a Peterson Tube). This is a piece of equipment used by all lifeguards to rescue casualties. Between Bilbo and the rescue tube is 2 meters (6 feet) of line which acts as a safety measure to stop the casualty from climbing onto Bilbo during the rescue. Bilbo swims around the person in distress, drawing the tube close to them. When Bilbo feels their weight clutching the tube, he knows it is time to turn round and swim back to the beach.

And yes, he has rescued people and prevented them from going into the sea when it was dangerous and unpredictable.

So what makes

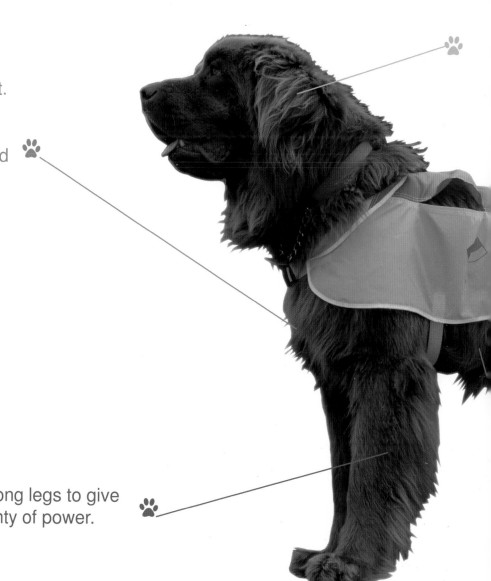

Bilbo has a double coat. The one on top is waterproof, and underneath a fine haired coat keeps him warm.

Bilbo has long legs to give him plenty of power.

Bilbo so special?

When Bilbo swims his ears stick flat, like big flaps to his head, which is perfect when he goes through the surf, since this prevents water from getting into his ears.

Bilbo has a big tail that acts like a rudder when he's swimming in the water.

Bilbo has amazingly big webs on his feet, which are like massive paddles to propel him along in the water.

Bilbo has extra large lungs which give him lots of endurance.

Hound hailed a hero after surf danger warning

During one trip that Jmo and Bilbo made to check the buoyancy aid of a remote cove close to Land's End, a woman walked past with a towel under her arm. Jmo asked the woman "you're not thinking of going into the sea are you?" She said yes and so he advised her not to do so, and explained that the sea had changed from the previous day and there was a strong swell running, making it dangerous for anybody to go in the water, let alone swim safely. But the woman ignored Jmo's advice and headed for the water's edge.

Without any prompting whatsoever, Bilbo sensed that she was going to get into the sea, and he simply took off spontaneously and ran back down the cliff path towards the woman on the beach placing himself between her and the sea, actually standing on her feet. She shouted for Jmo to tell his dog to go away, but Bilbo would not go away and tried to prevent her from entering the sea.

However the woman pushed past Bilbo, whereupon he raced into the surf to block her way. Only then did she realise how strong the current was, as she saw what a difficult time Bilbo was having in the powerful waves, so she did not go in. Bilbo had done his job!

Ever since Bilbo's first summer working on the beach in 2006, his popularity has just grown and grown. People love to visit him and see him patrolling his beach, and they travel from all over the world. Jmo has done many radio interviews nationwide to talk about his special dog, and TV crews have filmed Bilbo in action, and he has been televised around the world doing his rescues in the surf down at Sennen Cove. Bilbo was even featured on BBC1, Channel 4 and The Animal Planet.

So when Head Lifeguard Jmo visits schools to do talks and demonstrations, Bilbo goes with him. The children never forget the message of '*Swim Between The Flags*' when the large and beautiful chocolate coloured Newfoundland turns up in their classroom! Bilbo has become a very special educational tool for the Lifeguard Service since children can relate to him. Bilbo is so popular with children in schools that teachers have done projects and created wonderful classroom wall displays, with Bilbo and the Lifeguard Service as the central theme.

Did You Know ?

Bilbo originates from Newfoundland in Canada where his breed is well adapted to cope with the harsh cold water of the Labrador Current.

Bilbo knows his commands and is trained to Sit, Stay, and Wait. He even recognises some hand signals such as 'Come Back' and 'Stand Still'.

Bilbo is naturally chocolate coloured, but when he is on the beach in the summer his coat becomes quite bleached by the sun and salt water. In the winter his natural rich chocolate colour comes back. Interestingly Bilbo has four brothers and sisters, all with black fur — he was the only one born chocolate coloured!

Bilbo is 14 stones. You wouldn't know it from what he eats, since his food intake is not that huge really. For breakfast he might have some cereal with milk or yoghurt. For lunch some of his special dried food mixed with a smoked mackerel or raw egg. In the evening he'll be offered a large bowl of his special dried food with plenty of water. Bilbo likes to eat little and often and it's he who decides what he wants to eat!

Bilbo gets invited to open special events locally and around the county of Cornwall, and was invited to a prestigious Dog charity jamboree event in Devon where he performed 3 – 4 rescues in a lake and quite stole the show!

First thing in the morning Bilbo comes into Jmo's room and appears to smile and then he sits in front of Jmo. Jmo then asks *"Where's my kiss for the day?"* and Bilbo gives him a big slobbery kiss.

Bilbo measures horizontally nose to tip of tail 170 cm. He measures head to paw vertically 92 cm.

Crufts

N.E.C. BIRMINGHAM
8th, 9th, 10th, 11th
March 2007

Bilbo was the first and only ever dog to complete the Annual Newlyn to Penzance Open Water Swim of 1 mile. He did it in a time of 31minutes and 2 seconds.

Bilbo has been sponsored by a large dog food company who provide him with good quality dog food. They invited him to Crufts as part of a 'Dog Protection Team' for their exhibition stand, where a DVD clip played of Bilbo doing his rescues in the sea. He was given his own 'all expenses paid' hotel room! Bilbo proved a bit hit at Crufts.

People of all ages love Bilbo. One elderly lady who lives in a nursing home wrote to Jmo asking for a poster of Bilbo to put up in the communal sitting room, since all the residents admire Bilbo so much. He brightens everyone's day!

Bilbo even receives fan mail, and he has received presents in the post from people all over the world.

We love Bilbo!

Bilbo's Gallery

KNOW YOUR FLAGS

Red and yellow flags mark areas of water that are patrolled by lifeguards. These are the safest places to swim.

The red flag indicates danger. Never enter the water when the red flag is flying.

Black and white chequered flags indicate an area of water marked for use by craft. For your own safety, do not swim in these zones.

An orange windsock flying at the beach indicates that wind conditions are especially dangerous Under no circumstances should you take an inflatable into the sea.

With over 250,000 people visiting Sennen's mile long beach each year, Bilbo certainly has a very important role to fulfil in getting the message across about beach and water safety. People love to see him wearing his distinctive lifeguard jacket. The level of education he can deliver is outstanding, and the fact that he puts a smile on peoples' faces proves he is one very special and talented dog indeed. We hope you will agree!